FRESHWATER FIS[H]

COLOURING BOOK

BY YASMINE DAVEY

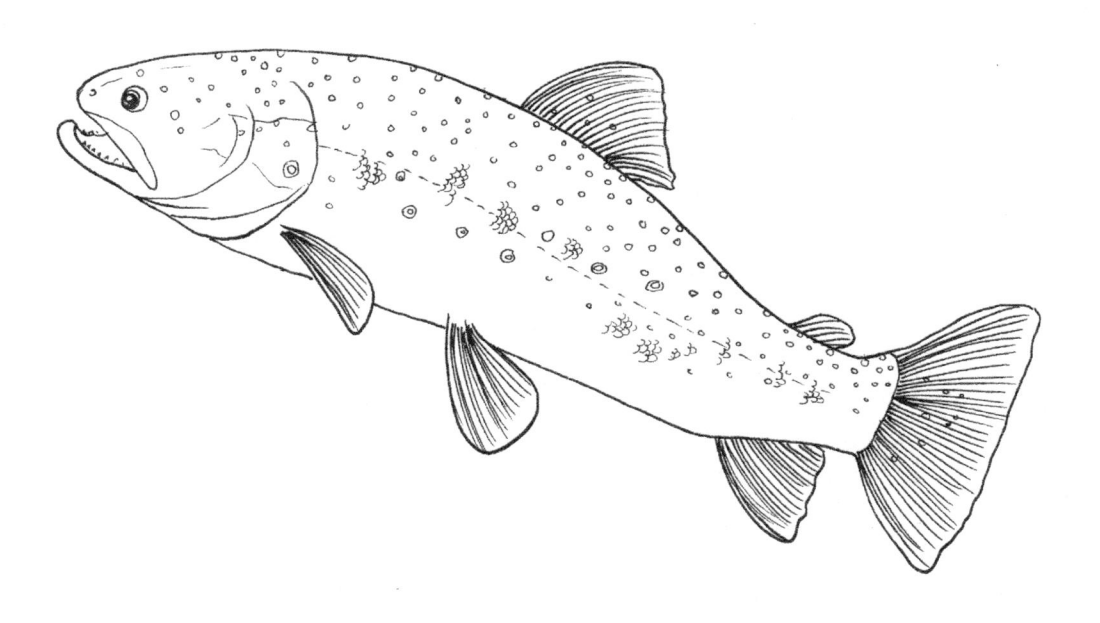

Copyright 2019
All rights reserved to
Sea Dancer Yasmine Davey

For my little fisherman and my mermaid

Copyright © 2019 by Yasmine Davey
All rights reserved. No part of this publication may be reproduced, distributed, or transmitted in any form or by any means, including photocopying, recording, or other electronic or mechanical methods, without the prior written permission of the publisher, except in the case of brief quotations embodied in critical reviews and certain other noncommercial uses permitted by copyright law. For permission requests, write to the publisher at : davey.jasmine@gmail.com.

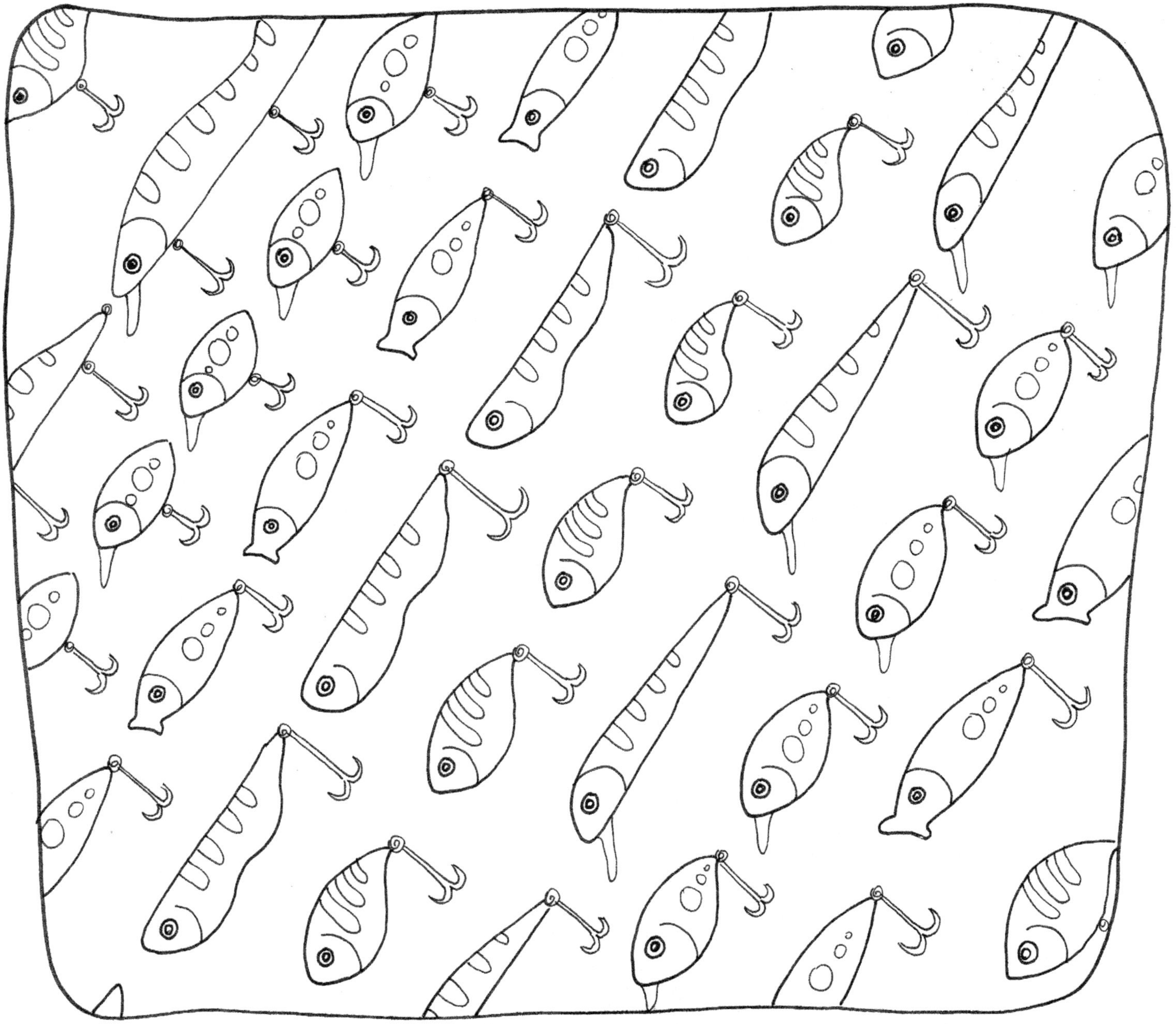

BREAM

BROWN TROUT

CHUB

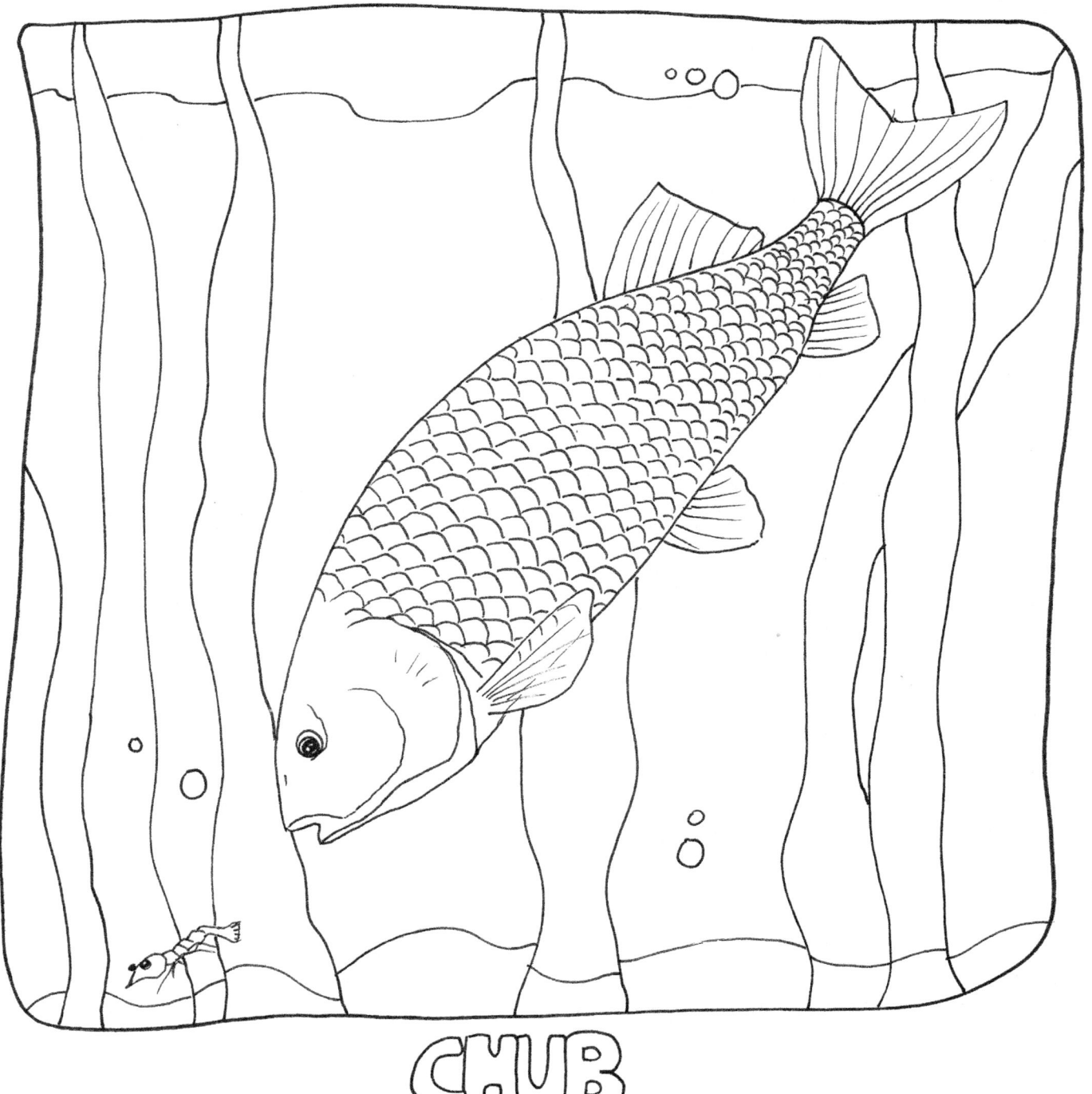

CRUCIAN CARP

DACE

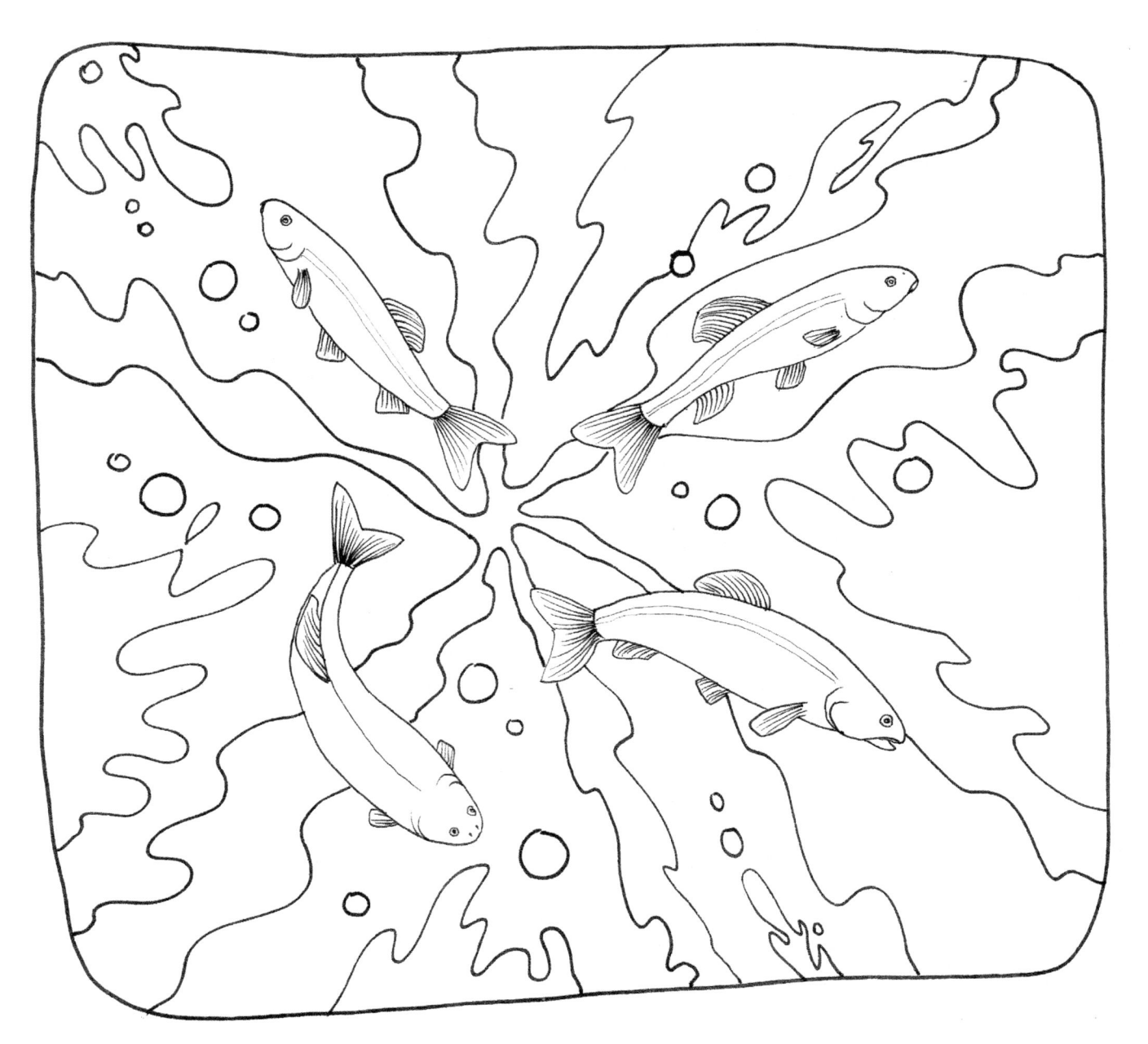

MINNOW

MIRROR CARP

NORTHEN PIKE

PERCH

RAINBOW TROUT

ROACH

RUDD

TENCH

WILD CARP

GRAYLING

BARBEL

BLEAK

ZANDER

BOWFIN

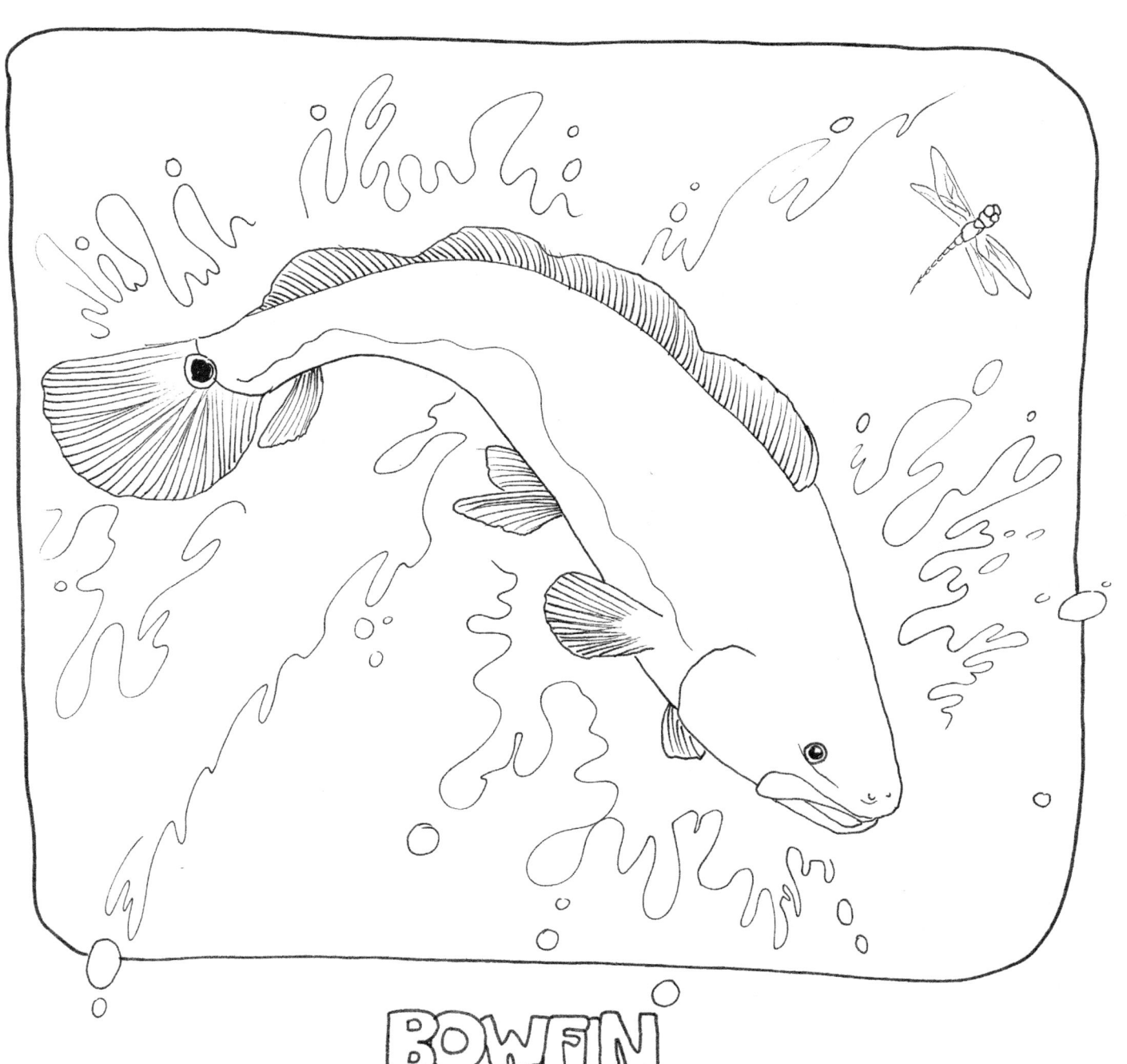

CHINOOK SALMON

ALLIGATOR GAR

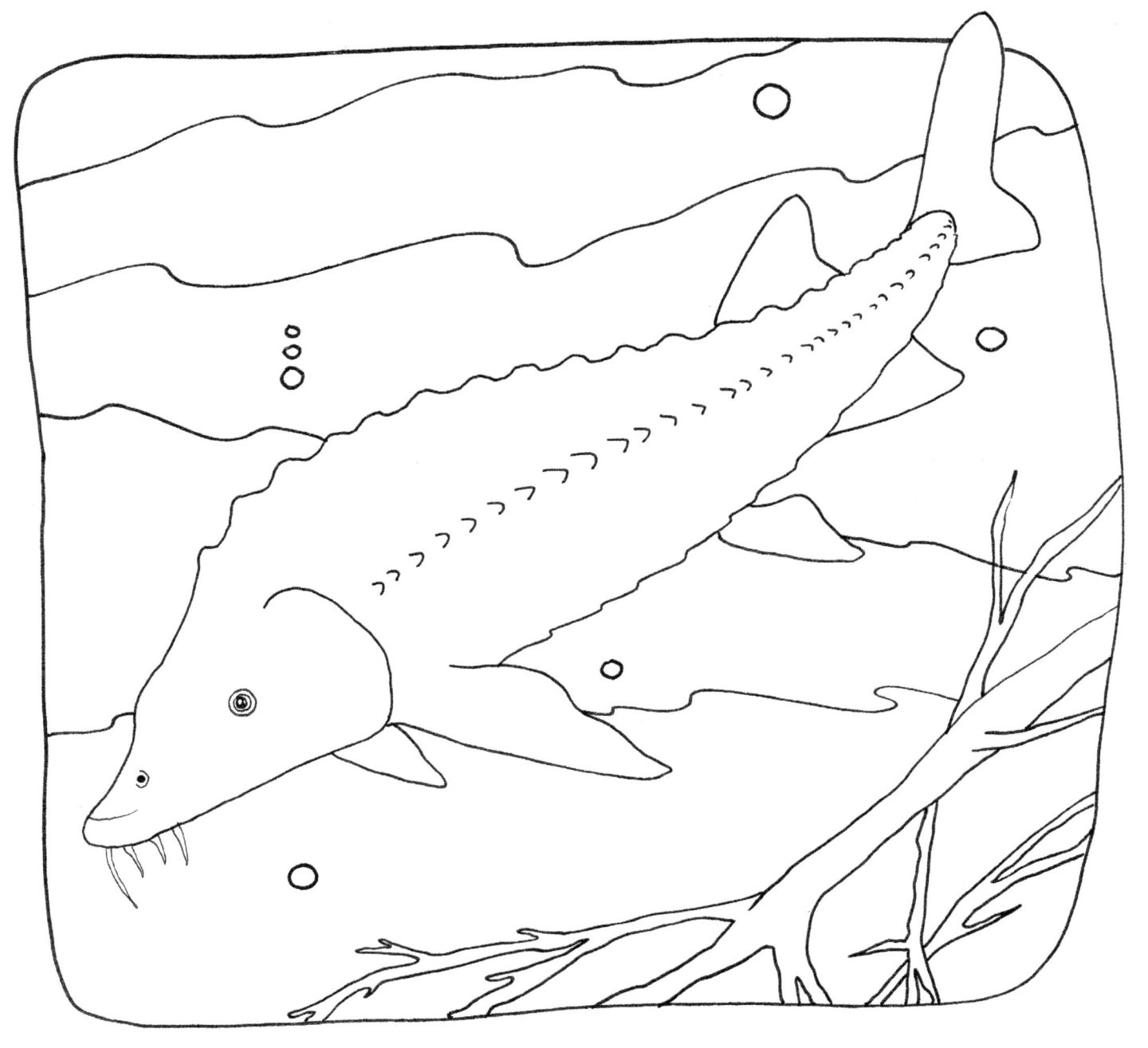

STURGEON

SNAKEHEAD

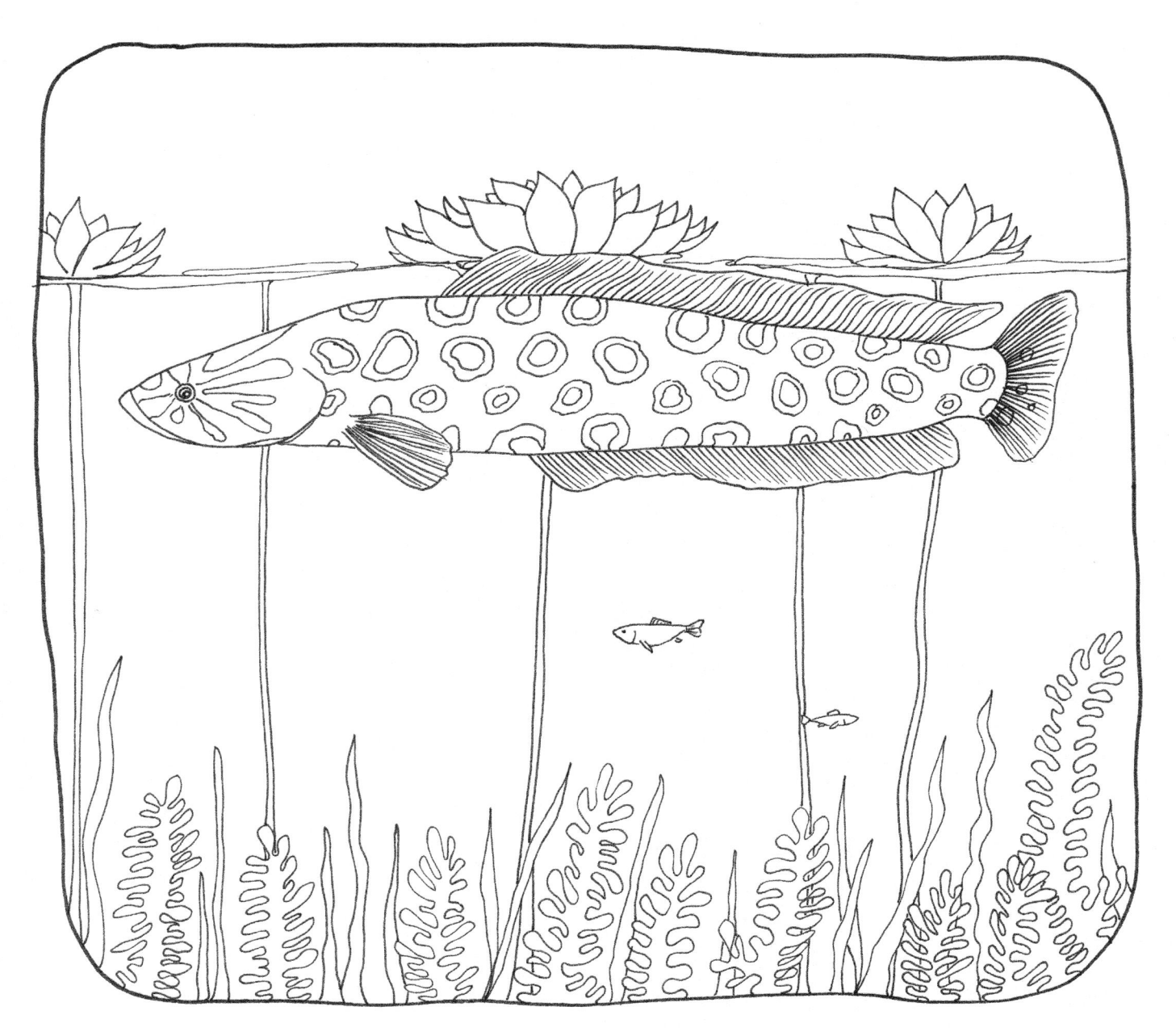

PEACOCK BASS

MURRAY COD

LARGEMOUTH BASS

GOLDEN DORADO

BLUE CATFISH

BLACK CRAPPIE

AROWANA

ARAPAIMA

GOLIATH TIGER FISH

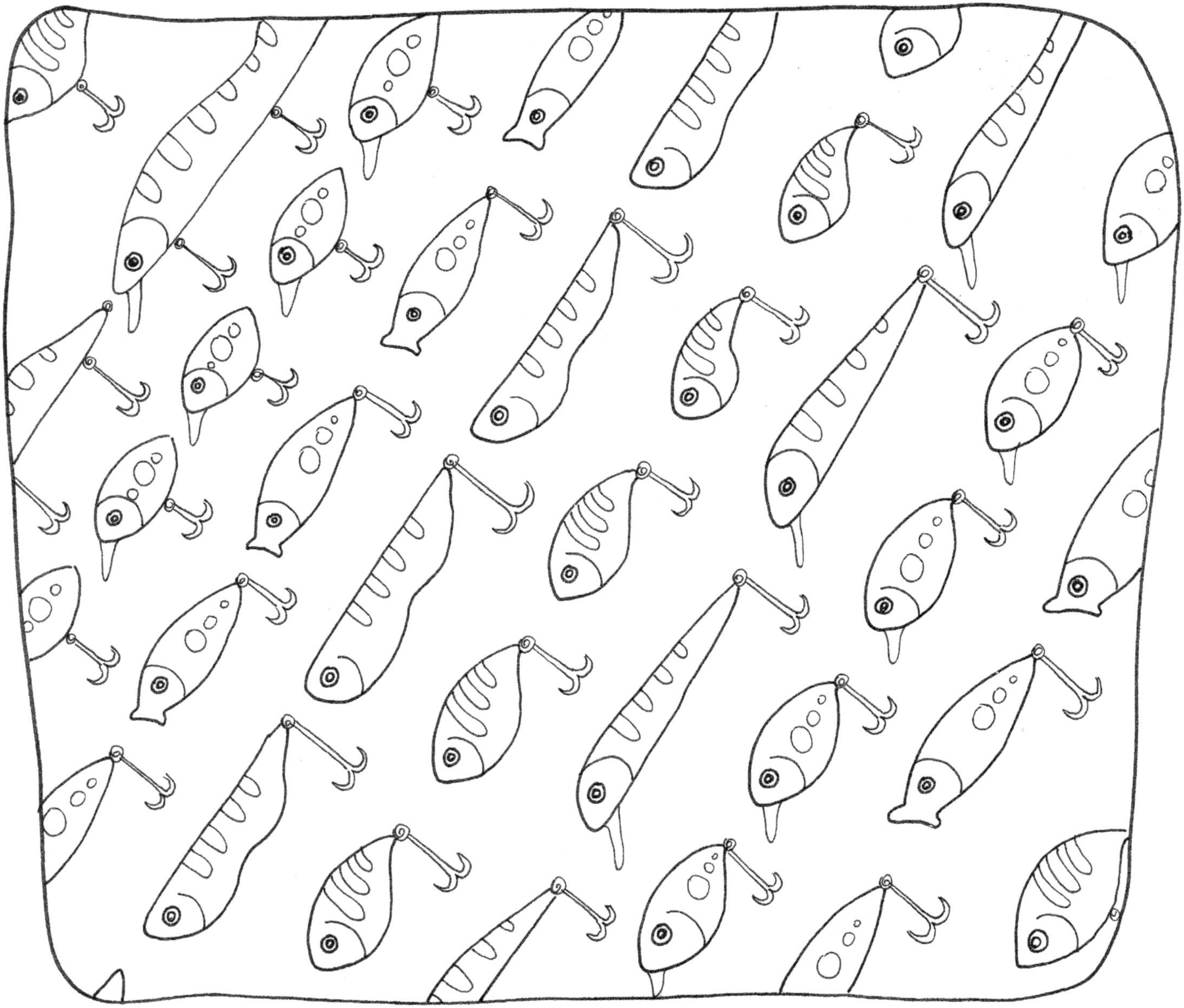

Printed in Great Britain
by Amazon